MORE THAN A CONQUEROR!

Jacqueline Scott

HOV
PUBLISHING

More Than A Conqueror!

HOV Publishing a division of HOV, LLC.
www.hovpub.com
hopeofvision@gmail.com

Cover Design: Hope of Vision Designs
Editor/Proofread: HOV Publishing

Contact the Author, Jacqueline Scott at:
jackiescott092@gmail.com

For further information regarding special discounts on bulk purchases, please visit www.hovpub.com

ISBN Paperback: 978-1-942871-64-4
ISBN eBook: 978-1-942871-65-1

10 9 8 7 6 5 4 3 2 1

Printed in the United States of America

Dedication

This book is dedicated to my family, my daughters
and friends. I am grateful to God for all my
accomplishments.

*Nay, in all these things we are more than conquerors
through him that loved us ~ Romans 8:37*

As stated in Ecclesiastes 9:11; The race is not given
to the swift nor the strong, but to those who can
endure to the end.

Introduction

As I share my stories of overcoming and conquering abandonment, healing becomes easier, and self-discovery continuously happens. The unconditional mercy and love that God has shown me inspired me to write this book. God is our Creator. Our life experiences are woven together so intricately that some of us may experience the same things but at different times and on different levels. Understanding this, led me to another reason for writing this book. I hope that by standing up in my own way, I can encourage people to keep going towards their dreams. We must continuously work on ourselves to transform and evolve into the best person we were created to be on this earth.

Several life experiences triggered me to deal with some deep-seeded pain in my own life. *God has not given us a spirit of fear, but of power and of love and of a sound mind* (2 Timothy 1:7). Writing this book allowed me to share the knowledge and understanding that I have gained about abandonment. In fact, the writing process became a spiritual journey. I had to look closely at my life choices. I had to heal myself, help the people I love and then to provide service to the world.

I have learned to lean on God and persevere through many of life's lessons. I choose to utilize this time dealing with the topic that God has placed on my heart. Abandonment. We can seek to motivate and inspire people with our life stories. Healing is needed on a global scale, and if we work together, we can make a difference. I began meeting people who, for one reason or another, experienced abandonment and I began to see that it was and still is a big issue. *This is where my story begins.*

Living in Harlem, New York, I felt like I always had to struggle and work hard to achieve success, and I did. God surely was in control. As I reflect on everything I have been through, I can see this clearly now, I am not a victim, but I am an overcomer.

Abandonment is a big issue. Unfortunately, I've lived through plenty of abandonment. and yet, by God's grace I have overcome it each time. I am grateful for having conquered many abandonment situations that were meant to break me, instead it made me wiser. I have even done some research and interviewed other people about their own abandonment experiences. I wanted to know their stories because this topic is so sensitive. It can transform your life...

Learning to love unconditionally is not easy. Although love is a feeling, like anything else, it must be taught in a healthy way. At times, we run from love, love of self. and even love from others. Sometimes, out of fear of change or fear of being hurt. Due to abandonment and not being able to love unconditionally can cause pain. That pain can push us to change. For example, through a conversation with one of my friends, I realized that he had never had the chance to just be a little boy. Having been forced to be a man early on in life and because of this, he still yearns for and is excited about the boy inside of him.

Through conversations with women and friends, I have also learned how we, as women, must have self-love to love others genuinely. Then, we as ladies must demand that people love us the way we love them and ourselves. I have come to this part of my life accepting and overcoming various abandonment situations. This whole writing process, journey of self-discovery (including the realization of how advocating for and loving others too much had left me feeling abandoned at times) and learning about others' experiences has left me feeling depleted yet fulfilled.

While writing down my feelings I saw this as a healing process. This process was to allow myself to reclaim who I am, rebuilding all the beauty and self-love that I had allowed to lay dormant inside of me for so long. I have become brave enough to share some true stories, facts, poems, thoughts, and suggestions on accepting, reflecting, and overcoming abandonment situations and the issues they have caused in our lives. I had to find a solution for addressing the residue of the abandonment issues I faced, one that would keep me physically and mentally healthy. I care about the quality of my life and yours, too. We owe it to ourselves to wake up every day feeling good. This is a feeling that can only come after dealing with the issues inside.

I love my relationship with God, and I am seeking Him in all things. I have been delivered from many trials and unpleasant experiences. I am grateful for my growth. I am NOT perfect, but I am definitely a better person. I have been delivered from things that no longer serve my higher good or me. I could not have made it without God. I had to believe that I was not one percent human but that I was a hundred percent human as I entered into and accepted God's mercy and grace. I began discovering and exploring my gift of empath and healing. The gifts of God are meant to enhance the kingdom of heaven. God activates our gifts, we pray and access the gifts according to Gods' will and purpose. I have grown humbly through my many life experiences and the guidance of the Holy Spirit Most importantly, I learned and grew in Jesus Christ. Studying on His biblical teachings of love and miraculous healing. I learned to heal and overcome situations that could have left me mentally unstable. Yes, being abandoned was difficult, but I am an overcomer. Having strong faith and perseverance to push through hard times was my answer.

Table of Contents

Chapter 1

Abandonment

Let's get to the root of things. As a child, I was abandoned. Then, later as an adult, I was again abandoned. It sounds like a pity party but it's not. Experiencing abandonment made me see some things. If not addressed as a child, the issue of abandonment can linger on into adulthood. Because of my own experiences with abandonment in my life, the topic of abandonment became an emotional and serious topic for me. As I began this writing journey, I started to think about how some of my life events may have helped shape me into the woman I am today. I also began thinking about how I could hear the Lord saying he wanted me to address other adults and kids who were orphaned and abandoned just like I was. Abandonment needs to be addressed, taught about, and openly discussed. Greater support and solutions need to be created. After this book, perhaps I can develop a curriculum targeting and resolving abandonment issues.

Abandonment, what is abandonment? Abandonment is the act of abandoning or leaving someone or something. Abandonment exists in many forms: abandonment of love, abandonment of animals, abandonment of people, abandonment of loved ones in death (pandemic), abandoned in jail, abandonment of veterans, abandonment of a location, abandonment of a class, abandonment of your children, abandonment of God, abandonment of self, feeling abandoned when a loved one dies, etc. Jesus, too, was abandoned. Despite the form of abandonment experienced, if abandonment issues are not thoroughly dealt with, they can produce dysfunction in the lives of those who experience them. If the abandonment experience is too traumatic, people can abandon parts of their lives altogether.

Some people have experienced mental illness because of abandonment. Others have experienced violence or may have caused violence after dealing with abandonment. For me, it was a silent reflection. Several times, I even felt the enemy of depression rising up. I was at a low point in my life. However, I am more than a conqueror through Christ Jesus. Romans 8:37 states, Although I went to counseling to deal with my issues, only my prayers and worship uplifted my spirit. My faith was strong and giving up was not an option.

Chapter 2
Testimonies

Many important events in my life have had a significant impact on me. However, I've realized over time that my tests were my testimonies and reflecting on the events that comprised my life story led me to the acceptance of my true self. Yes, I had to accept my mistakes. I had to accept the mistake of repeating the cycle of looking for love outside of myself first. I had to accept and acknowledge the mistake of putting others before myself to my detriment. There were just too many people pulling at my energy, leaving me abused, empty and abandoned most of the time.

In the end, I had developed a victim mentality, and I functioned like this until I realized that there were areas in my life that I needed to work on for things to be different. I went through a short period of blaming others. However, that did not last long because I knew what it was to have nothing. I started reflecting and realizing that I had accomplished so much in life. I knew that victory would be mine. I had to learn to fill my own cup and renew my faith in God. I had to remember that trouble wouldn't always last; better days would inevitably come.

The following are some of the events that changed my life in a significant way. There were lessons and blessings, some painful and some joyful, but ultimately, they all helped to shape me into who I am today.

Parent Abandonment

As a child, my biological parents abandoned my brothers and me. My name was and will always still be Jacqueline Ortiz Escalera. Jose Escalera and Joaquina Ortiz were my biological parents, the ones who birthed my brothers and I and then gave us up for adoption. It was a horrible experience and feeling knowing that our parents had left us behind and gone on with their lives. This was a confusing time for my brothers and me because we had to learn how to speak English. I was about six years old when they gave us up and being abandoned at such an early age left me so traumatized that I can barely remember my kindergarten through second-grade learning experience. However, I clearly recall being in a group home with a bunch of other kids. My not knowing English or understanding what was going on in my life was just something else to deal with as an abandoned child. However, it was an obstacle that I accepted and finally overcame. By the fifth grade, I was speaking English. Not fluently, but well enough to get by.

I remember driving to New York City from Middletown, New York and going to an agency named Pius XII. It was there that my brothers and I would visit with our mother. During our visit, she would look up at the ceiling instead of at us, as if looking at us was the hardest thing in the world for her to do. I was just happy to see her. Then, just like that, the visit was over and back to the group home we all went.

I never knew my father. I do remember going to Puerto Rico to watch my stepbrother, Alfredo Escalera. I recall Alfredo fighting in a boxing match, but that was the extent of our relationship. I was about three or four years old at the time. After I went upstate, I never saw my father again. All I remember was the feeling that I had no father and my mother seemed to not care. I had so many questions. Where was my mother going after leaving my brothers and me? I was shipped from group home to group home and to foster care homes. Thank God I was never abused – perhaps neglected a few times, but never abused. We kept moving from group home back to the group home, because my brothers would act up. We all would get sent back to the group home.

God blessed me to meet Evelyn and Edward Scott in 1974. They became my foster parents. At first, I would visit them on the weekends, Then for a whole week. A few years passed by, and they became my parents, adopting me in 1978. So many thoughts went through my mind. I never wanted to change my last name. I remember crying, saying, "No, I don't want to get adopted! I don't want to change my last name!" However, in order to get adopted, I had to change my name. Looking back, it was the best thing for me. With my new adoptive family, I grew up in a beautiful, stable home. Of course, not everything was perfect, but it was everything for a young girl who had nothing. Harlem World, here I am, Jacqueline Scott! Yet, I did not realize I was losing my Latino race and culture, like my friend Pamela Gomez Cyrus who we lost but she will never be forgotten. My other friend D and I hung out all the time and we are still in contact over 40 years later.

My parents instilled church in me and a feeling of devotion to family. God became my spiritual father, and Edward Scott became my physical father. I finally had a dad. I never wanted for anything in my new family. I was showered with love, fine clothing, furs jewelry, family functions, and trips. My mother was more of a disciplinarian, while my dad pampered us and did whatever mom needed him to do.

Unfortunately, my mother, Evelyn Scott, passed away from cancer, in 1989 and then my dad passed away in 1996.

Losing them both brought back that void and thoughts of my biological parents. I always wondered why my biological parents gave me up. The love that had helped me to grow up and nurture me was now gone. I thank God for the few church elders and community elders that were there to encourage me and talk with me. One who will always be dear to my heart is Beatrice Prioleau. Mother Prioleau was my mother's best friend. She would come to our house every Sunday, with T. T and A is my extended family and when my mother passed away, Mother Prioleau was there for me. She would give me great council and would always encourage me to go forward in the Lord. Mother Prioleau also played a big part in my daughter's lives. As she showered them with love and taught them to be independent and confident in who they were. Unfortunately, she moved to North Carolina and then passed away in 2021.

God has blessed me with a wonderful woman named Christine Riley. My kids call her godmommy Tina! She is my daughter Emkasias godmother. Tina is a pillar in the community, and I must say she has been a gift in my life. She has always been there for me and my children. While I attended school she babysat most of my daughters and has even taken care of my grandsons. I thank God for her love and continuous support.

I attended P.S. 171 in Manhattan. I sat in class and did not speak because I was busy learning English. At that time there were no Bilingual classes, and we learned a lot by memorization. I had my first fight in fourth grade, and I've been fighting ever since, not always physically, but fighting for what is right and best for me.

I continued to live my early years learning the English language. In middle school Jackie Robinson and high school Norman Thomas. I was met with various challenges, but none that negatively impacted me. I attended Alvin Alley Dance Company, The Big Apple Circus and Dance Company and sang in a choir. Back during that time in the 1980s, things were different. There were a lot more resources and programs for kids, especially activities and opportunities for children in the arts. Today, I look at how many school districts are trying to bring after school programs back, and I think about how fearful I was when I was younger. I had talent but was afraid to embrace it fully. Looking back, I feel that I should have gone further in one of those areas. Dance was my favorite. The truth is I was trying too hard to fit in. I occupied all this time with many activities. The activities were dance, gymnastics, and singing to name a few. I guess that I just swept the absence of my parents and lack of culture under the rug, covered it up and put it in a box so that it would not be addressed. Why? Because I felt abandoned by the people who should have loved me and did not fight to keep me: my biological parents.

Even though The Scotts loved me, I still felt a void. My brothers Jose, Robert and Luis, would visit me in New York City, but I didn't care to see them when they did. They always wanted something from me. Mother Scott would say, "Be nice to your brothers. They will need you one day." Boy, was she right. My brothers were my world, and they represented the only connection that I had to my true cultural self. Over time, I saw them less and less frequently. They started abandoning me, or so I thought. In reality, they were actually just living their own lives. However, as I was already feeling bad and constantly reflecting on how my parents just let us go, I internalized these feelings and built up a wall.

As a teenager, I enjoyed hanging out with my friends. Being outside exposed me to more things in the world that I had not experienced. However, I could not hang out late because Mom did not play that. When I was younger, I had never really cared about how boys felt, so I never got hurt. I would say that it was when I was about 16 years old that I started really liking boys

– but I treated them badly. I would fight them and beat them up, but they seemed to like it. I always felt like since I could fight, I was considered "down" with the fellas. At times, it was me taking my anger out on them. The anger that I felt for my dad allowed me to treat them poorly. Self-hatred was strong! I don't think I hated myself. The hate was towards my dad for not being there or explaining why it was that easy to dismiss his own flesh and blood. So, I took it out on the boys.

I learned that even though I did not have my biological parents that I was fortunate enough to have parents who raised me in a loving environment. Sometimes your blood family is just that. It took a long time for me to overcome the feeling of anger and confusion towards my biological parents, but it all worked out for my good.

Love Abandonment

My first true love, or so I thought, was a young boy named A.D. Don't get me wrong; it was a unique shared learning experience. We had great times before our relationship transformed and became toxic. Together, we produced a beautiful baby girl in 1986 when I was 18 years old. We were too young to know what was right and what we really wanted. I know that God provides because He allowed me to be strong and independent. I worked in real estate and got my first apartment in Harlem. Not wanting to abandon my daughter, I worked really hard to take care of her. I got my own apartment at 19 years old and had a strong independence about myself. I just remember praying a lot for guidance, wisdom, knowledge and understanding.

Unfortunately, A.D. and I parted ways due to toxic behaviors. The verbal abuse that I had endured from him did not last long. I lost it one day: I cut him and walked away with my child. I dated very little at this time, but I partied like a rock star every weekend with my gals Sabrina, and Janice. I still say that God was taking care of this fool right here! I never lost focus on my career, child, or education. This was a good time in my life. I was a young lady, had my own apartment and a job, and was going to the College of New Rochelle.

In 1993, I met and married E.M. This relationship started slowly, and then it picked up. It was full of excitement and love. We talked for hours and encouraged each other to be the best we could be. It's important to give credit where it was due. As time passed, our relationship grew, and we wanted to be together. As I look back now, I realize that I was the aggressive one when it came to getting married because I didn't want to playhouse. We got married on July 28, 2006, and life was great! He was a great father to my daughter Alacea. I already had my own apartment, a job, and I was attending school.

I graduated in 1995 from the College of New Rochelle with a 3.8 GPA. We both were excited because we were about to be parents together. I was graduating and having a baby in the same year. Emkasia was in my womb, and I finally felt like I could trust someone with my love. E.M. worked and still works for the NYC Transit Department. I was working and still work for the Board of Education and could not wait for the summertime to come. E.M. and I went on dates and enjoyed parties every weekend. These years between the 1990s and the 2000's were some of the best times of my life. Our family would go down south to Virginia every year, where we would attend a family reunion in Virginia that happened every third week in July.

Love was steadily growing. In May of 2001, I had a beautiful baby girl named Jasmond. I had no complaints, and we were thriving as a family. We attended church, community cookouts, and we all enjoyed our family events.

Eventually, after about a good 12 years, the reality of marriage set in. Things changed: life, friends, situations and even statuses. That could be a whole other book. At this time, I was still working for the city and enjoying it. I was growing, and so many positive events were taking place. I was learning to be a great teacher. Yet, I still did things a bit out of character when it came to my personal goals. I enrolled in Cambridge College for my master's degree. In June of 2006, our last daughter, Monajae, was born. I was successful, but things were shifting in the marriage. After years of going on family trips, enjoying community cookouts and feeling like we didn't need anything else, we got too comfortable. We would go down every summer to my ex-husband family land that he co-owns. I would mention how we could build a house on the property or a store down the road. I started feeling like I wanted more. I wanted a house on the land, and it just did not happen. I started being comfy and lazy. I settled for what he had at that time because we really did not need anything. Church became my go to place. This is where I grew spiritually. Without council we just spent money and lived life without future hopes. I actually ignored my true desire for more for myself. I was grateful. Deep down I expected more. They say idol time is the devil's playground. We started indulging in smoking and drinking. Which is not anything uncommon at that time.

Around 2013, our marriage had taken a turn for the worse due to infidelity. It's okay; it happens to the best of us. It's just life. That is why it is important to be equally yoked with someone. You have to at least be aligned with or on the same vibrational level as your partner in order to grow. In my marriage, our goals were not the same. I did seek counseling for our marriage, but it did not work. Relationships are meant to grow. Infidelity started to play a part in the relationship, and after a few years, my ex-husband moved out. I waited for way too long to separate. After that, I lost myself in other relationships and affairs that followed the same patterns. I stayed on this rollercoaster ride until I'd had enough: I separated from my husband, and then we got divorced. I finally had FREEEDOM... or so I thought. Freedom to explore and still be unclear of my purpose.

I had abandoned my self-worth and myself all in the name of love. In the name of marital love. love that was not growing. Thank God I snapped out of that and filed for a divorce in 2019. I'd never wanted to be divorced, but God did not want me to sit in the mess of loneliness and repeated cycles of behavior that did not help me grow. My purpose was greater than I knew, and it had to be fulfilled. People watched to see how I would respond to my divorce. Would I be so broken that I could not recover? Did I truly trust in God? Yes, I did, and I walked in that truth. I still have love for my ex-spouse and wish the best for him. I pray that my kids see that I turned to God and that He guided me through. However, that was not the most powerful marital love I have ever felt. I sacrificed that love because it was forbidden. The Law of God is covered in the New Testament, but it is still true, and karma is real.

Loving a person that was not for me is something that I said I would never do, but somehow, it happened. I met this man who I felt was everything I ever could want, but he was married. *Sheesh*…the ultimate test, and I had failed. The lesson caused me to walk away from a lot of people, places, and things. I had to walk away from some of my own family members. This was hard because I never wanted them to know that feeling of being abandoned. It was like a band aid was ripped off an unhealed wound...my heart. God's love is the only reason that I have not shared the names of the people; true love, which is *agape* love, covers a multitude of sins. The pain of abandonment and betrayal rose up in me like a flood and it forced me to pray and look within. This catapulted me into higher self-worth – an ascension like no other – and a greater understanding of myself with more self-love. The ascension does require sacrifice. Self-care to heal from pain that can be hard to explain or even understand. Honestly, I cried and pressed my way. Pleading for the holy spirit to fill me with overflowing love for myself. Sometimes a person's rejection is God's protection.

Abandonment on a Job

This book came after a whole lot of praying, worshipping, and working at a job that I loved with all my heart. Let's talk about that abandonment. Working was everything to me, and yet I watched people abandon me at a job that I had been working at for 15 years at the time. But God. Hallelujah! It was during this season that I had to learn how to protect my heart and my mind.

How do you work for a government, city agency, private company, etc., for so many years, only to be easily discarded or abandoned without any compassion or care? As a teacher It is our responsibility to provide the best education for students, I advocated for students who had a need for special educational services. Advocating for others can leave many of us abused and feeling misunderstood. Yet, the greatest feeling is knowing that through your advocacy, a difference was made in a child's or a person's life. I know I fought so hard for them because I was abandoned and was not going to sit around and watch them not get their services. Unfortunately, I had to go to court with a job I loved and did every day with great passion. I started working for the City of New York in 1999 and have worked there for more than 23 years. Today, I still walk into the classroom, look at those beautiful kids, and love them like my own. Teaching children has brought great joy into my life.

In 2016, after about 16 years on the job, things began to change. First, it was an organizational name changed from B.O.E. to D.O.E. Then, the changes trickled into the schools. This is where I learned that actions speak louder than words as my life took a challenging turn. You can say lot of things but what you do is all people see. If you sit by and watch people being treated unfairly that makes you a bystander. When I became an advocate for special education children, I paid a heavy price for defending what I knew they needed. In doing so, I ended up becoming a target for dismissal and the attacks began. I was wrongly accused of things and of not doing my job, to put it nicely. I will not mention names, for it does me no good to judge others. For the Lord says, "*Judge not lest ye be judged*" (Matthew 7:1). Friends said that I should have sued, but instead, I pressed on because I knew that God had protected me and brought me out on top before.

I became ill. After having to go to court for a whole year, I was stressed out, and my body and mind had been wounded. I felt very isolated and heartbroken. I was abandoned by many of my co-workers. Honestly, no one goes against the administration in the organization where I work, so co-workers became bystanders. They watched people lose their jobs and so did I. People lost their jobs or were forced to retire earlier than they would have liked. When my turn came for the advisory board to destroy that which I had worked so hard for (my career), a few people encouraged me, but many stood by and just watched. In the end, my illness got worse. I would go to work sick every day and was scared that I would lose my job. I was doing everything I was told so that I would be in compliance. I trusted God, and I realize now when I look back that God was protecting me.

The Holy Spirit and my perseverance kept me going. I would go to work and sit in the library listening to gospel music, and I would clean up the library as well. I was still amazing, even at this job. I am sure a lot of people who watched me go through were wondering how I did it. I was being devalued and it was horrible. Looking back, I was stronger than I even knew. A friend, C.B., encouraged me to fight and not give up. She would say, "Scott, you are like twine. They cannot break you!" It was true, and I walked in that belief and in my faith. Through all of this I was hurt. I had to get a personal lawyer D.M. He was excellent and we won!!

I went to court for about 13 days, which stretched out over an entire year. I endured this experience while going through a separation, attending Manhattan Bible Institute, servicing the community, singing, and participating in ministries at my church, Paradise Baptist Church, and taking care of my kids. My mind was strong, but my body took the hit: hypertension, weight loss and a breast cancer scare. I would be at work sick, and then I started missing days at work. Eventually, I had to take a leave of absence from my job. It was exactly what I needed. I rested and was strengthening my walk with God. However, the world and my vices would be another crutch.

Before long, it was time to go back to work, but I was in a fog. That's when everything hit the fan. I was having way too much fun and not really paying attention to the call on my life. I started having a couple of adulterous affairs. I hid them because I knew deep down that it was not what I wanted to do, but they sure made me feel good and cared for at the time.

I had never taken a leave of absence from my job before, so I had not been informed of all the stipulations. The information that I received allowed me to take my leave with pay, or so I thought. As it turned out, this was not the case. Eventually, the UFT and the payroll department realized that I had not been taken off the payroll during my leave. When they learned of this error, they came to get that money back. I ended up paying back about $20,000. I know that God kept me through it all. I was not supposed to get paid, but God made it so. If I had been taken off the payroll, I would have been HOMELESS!

Hallelujah to my sustainer, protector and Savior, God! God made it where I had gotten paid while I was sick and at home. I tried to explain to my family that I had fallen on hard times. However, they just looked at me as if to say, "You are lying." After that, I suffered in silence. I guess that my family was so used to me having money that it was hard to believe that things had really changed. However, when Christmas 2019 came, and there were no gifts from me under the tree, reality hit them. Not having money made no difference to me; I already knew what it felt like to have nothing. My family, on the other hand, was different; they had gotten used to the good life. The impact that the change in my finances had on my family caused me more stress, and then the isolation began. I abandoned myself. I could not see myself anymore. Self-esteem and confidence are so important to navigating in life. Holding on to them is what helped me refuse to give up this fight.

I started looking at my life, all that I had endured, and the fact that I still worshiped and praised God every day. I stood up for myself, and we won the court case. I was placed back in my position at work, so happy and grateful to have a job. Do you see the work of God and the grace and mercy that He bestowed upon me?

Still, I was not seeing clearly. God caused me to be still. I was not treated fairly, and I was allowing it because I still had not dealt with all of the destructive things in my life. However, rather than waste it, I turned all of this pain into action. During this time of my life, I grew in church and my spiritual gifts started manifesting. I enjoyed the church and loved the feeling of knowing God and Christ. The Holy Spirit was working with me.

I love my pastor, Dr. Rev. Lee A. Arrington, and my church family. I have learned the gospel from pastors preaching on Sundays. My love of gospel music ministry grew from participating in the choirs at Paradise Baptist Church. The Youth choir, Mass Choir and Choir #2. I am a worshiper, and I am proud to say that. I love music, in general. Also, the Manhattan Bible Institute has broadened my understanding of theology. Great teachers, pastors, evangelists, and bishops have helped me to go from milk to meat in the Bible, I have learned that God is love, and love covers a multitude of sin. I have also learned that energy is always present and that good and evil reside in all of us; the choices that we make while we are learning are what make the difference. Our gifts make room for learning and continuous growth. Our negative behaviors cause sin and great karmic consequences to our lives on this earth. I wonder what happens in the heavens when we who are the light of the world (the church) are not growing and ascending in Christ/God. Because some people have been indoctrinated, they do not want to see other people's religion or church history. That is like saying, "I don't want to know or learn about any other culture, food or any other country but my own." Where is the growth in that? All I hear God saying is, "Preach the gospel," and to grow to be the best version of myself. It is bigger than one person. We are here to help each other grow, too.

Abandonment at Death
Here Today Gone Tomorrow: Pandemic 2020

As I am writing this book, I am living through a pandemic: COVID-19. There were so many people who died from the disease all alone. It grieved my heart to see the world suffering in this way. I created a song entitled "Gone but Never Forgotten" in memory of all who passed away during that time. I also interviewed my friend along with a few other people.

Many people felt it was too difficult to talk about because people were passing away so quickly. I spoke with a friend of mine named Janice Key. Her mother, Ethera Key, was born in 1942. Ethera passed away on April 7, 2020, from COVID-19. Ethera had underlying health issues that included lung cancer, and in the lungs is where COVID-19 resides. Unfortunately, Ethera's lungs were not strong enough to fight COVID-19. COVID-19 snuck up on her, and then things went very quickly. I am so sorry for my friend's loss. Many people lost loved ones during this time due to this deadly Virus Covid-19. I asked Janice some questions and I could see it was difficult for her. I could feel her pain, as I had suffered some losses during the Pandemic.

"All I can say is I am so hurt. I can't believe this. This has put a strain on my relationship with my sister. It was so shocking that it all happened so fast. I had all of my mother's belongings." I said to Janice, "I am so saddened to hear of the loss." All I remember doing was praying for Janice at that moment. I also, continuously pray for all those who have lost loved ones during this Pandemic.

Chapter 3
Big On God

I began writing this book two years ago by writing my thoughts down weekly. The topic of abandonment came to me during the global pandemic of 2020, which took more than 500,000 lives in the U.S. alone. I endured the pandemic in New York City, one of the areas hardest hit by COVID-19.

During the pandemic, the Lord was showing me who I was outside of the church. My brother in Christ had passed away, and our church had a major flood. I started to look at what was most important to me. Although I had attended church as a child, I had taken a break as an adult, just living life. After being motivated to do so by my daughter and her godmother, eventually, I went back to church. Upon my return, I knew that I had a spirit of worship and praise. I started yearning to learn more about God and Jesus. Praying to God is what I had always done, but I had not prayed to Jesus. I really learned to study to show myself approved unto God and not man when I began attending the Manhattan Bible Institute. There was this tugging in my heart as I prayed and worshiped every Sunday.

My pastor, Dr. Rev. Lee A. Arrington, the shepherd at Paradise Baptist Church, is both a God-fearing man and my spiritual father. The elders in my church and other awesome preachers and teachers were delivering the gospel from the Bible and motivation. I just wanted to learn more. I see now that minorities have been taught the part of the Bible that was meant to keep them enslaved. The books of Psalms and Proverbs are very enlightening along with the many stories of overcomers in the Bible. We should look to the many great pioneers and historians in the world and Bible who made a difference and overcame many obstacles to do so.

The Lord had shown His strength and loyalty so many times in my life that I had to praise Him. I felt compelled to worship Him even if people could not understand my loyalty and dedication to a God that they could not see, yet I could feel. I sang in the church choir. This made it easy for me to do what I already felt in my soul. My brother, Bobby Arrington, who was the minister of music at my church, made me sing lead. I suppose that that is when the anointing started to fall upon me. The Sundays turned into almost every day of listening to gospel music, worshiping, and praising.

Anyone knows that as you begin to grow in positivity, negativity is never far behind. Instead of being supportive, people will often become jealous, nosey, envious, and bitter, which are poisonous to your growth, especially when things are feeling so great. At the time, I was so naïve, and I was too trusting. People saw that and took advantage of it. Yet, I refused to play the victim. My faith in God grew even more after I cried my heart out. Through this experience, I learned that we cannot play with non-believers. Although it is not our job to judge them, our words can convict and prick their hearts to consider change. Only God can save through Christ.

Opening yourself up to learning and embracing God's word is the start. I am spiritual, but I realized that I did not want to be indoctrinated. I had no problem learning of other people's culture, history and contributions to the community, to the world and to history. However, in opening up to being taught the things of God, I had to adapt to a whole biblical culture that was not mine. When we do not want to see other people's religion, perspectives, or church history, how do we learn? Where's the growth in that? The realization of this only made me want to learn more. It led me to begin attending Manhattan Bible Institute. Since enrolling, I have learned more about theology than I ever thought possible. The Bible instructs us, *"Study to show thyself approved unto God, a workman needeth not be ashamed, rightly dividing the word of truth"* (2 Timothy 2:15).

Chapter 4

The Beginning Of The End
(Poems)

I include original poetry and affirmations in this part of the book. I wrote them when I was at a low point in my life. This was the beginning of the end. I had to reflect on my self-doubt, of not trusting people, of giving myself to people who do not serve my higher good, of relationships that were not reciprocated and of friendships, which was the hardest thing for me. I wanted to take everyone along with me in this process, but this was a gift God had just for me. I was learning and understanding that people who are broken and hurt will hurt other people, sometimes intentionally and sometimes unintentionally. I had suffered long enough, and then God started blessing me.

There are doors that God opens that no man can shut. Meaning, certain people, places, and things had to be ended, so I could walk into a better destiny for myself. In my spirit, I knew that God would do what He said He would do in His word. He would supply all of my needs according to His riches in glory (Philippians 4:19). He would hide me behind the cross. He would be my shield and buckler. Then, one of my favorite scriptures tells me that He would cover me: *"He that dwelleth in the secret place of the Most High shall abide under the shadow of the Almighty"* (Psalm 91:1). I started reflecting on these promises, speaking life over myself and healing. I am here to win, adding positive value and growth to my life daily.

"ACCEPT IT!"

I have accepted…

GOD, healing, life, hurt, betrayal, love, loyalty, criticism, yourself (myself), loneliness, love, healing, strength, learning, shifts, eagerness, power, trust, releasing, and information.

Please feel free to add what you know needs to be accepted in your own life.

I am grateful for…

Love, my life, the Trinity (God, Christ, Holy Spirit), ancestors, archangels, wisdom, knowledge, understanding, mistakes, protection, kids (my daughters/grandsons), shelter, food, my car, job, clothing, extended family, friends, leaders, and teachers who helped me grow, Edward and Evelyn Scott, money for bills, my brothers and sisters, a sound mind, strength, anointing, nature and perseverance.

WHY?

Why do we cry?

Why do we go?

Why do we lie?

Why do we sing?

Why do we die?

Why do we leave?

Why do we cheat?

Why do we stay?

Why do we care?

Why do we learn?

Why do we love?

Why do we release?

Why do we change?

Why do we try?

Why do we blame?

Why do we feel?

Why do we worry?

Why do we chase?

Why?

Chapter 5

My Work Is Not Done

I must work the works of him that sent me, while it is day; the night cometh, when no man can work.

John 9:4 KJV

In conclusion, nothing catches God off guard, and nothing will hold me back. I heard God say, "Jackie, in your nakedness, I see who you are." "Naked" meaning broken down in my spirit and at my lowest point. I had to renew my love for Christ. I had my faith tested. Remember, God is the light in darkness, therefore we are the light as well. I also learned that I could not get comfortable in sin. Our sin is in our flesh. One of my professors said, "Sin will take you further than you want to go and keep you there longer than you want to be." The Bible says that in our flesh dwells no good thing (Romans 7:18). So, sometimes, when we want to do what is right, our weak flesh will do its own thing. Instead of worrying, we should worship, pray reflect and work on ourselves. This is what I did to conquer my shadows of fear, lust, envy, anger, sadness, worry and a lack mentality, The many mountains in my life forced me to confront myself, overcome some situations, and transforming my mind.

Confronting myself was not easy, but it was a necessary part of the transformation. As God heals and delivers us, we can use other resources on this to help us fill our own cups. Forgiveness was for me. No one has to apologize for anything they did to me in the past as long as God keeps me. The scripture says, "*While we were yet sinners Christ died for us*" (Romans 5:8).

I had to accept the mistakes I made when repeating a cycle of looking for love outside of myself. Even forgiving myself for unintentionally hurting people and looking for other people's validation and love. I also had to see that putting others before myself for so long was becoming detrimental. I looked like a victim because I allowed myself to be abused and then abandoned. Once I reflected and healed, I put forth actions to change things and make life better. I ended up surrendering to God, for I had nothing left to give.

The peace of God is great for the soul. It is obtained when accepting and learning the lessons which helps us to heal, grow, and in turn, we can help others. We must change how we live and think. A lot of times, we speak words, and yet we are saying nothing. I had to let my story be heard. I had to learn not to be offended by what people say. I had to show myself the love that I was showing everyone else. I had to be honest with myself and remember who I was in Christ, overcoming any negative feelings that the past abandonments of my life caused me to feel. I had to release all the one-sided relationships in my life. I had to release being the "chaser," going after others to have a relationship with me due to my fear of abandonment. I also had to stick to my decisions after making healthy choices, not going back, and changing my mind because some people love bombed me so well. Love bombing is pretending to like someone more than you do. This was a trigger for me, and it brought me back to a level of sadness from which I was meant to move away.

Chapter 6

More Than Conquerors
Restoration & Personal Resources

We are more than conquerors in Christ Jesus (Romans 8:37)! God tells us this in His word. It was the uplifting words that I found in the Bible that kept me. I would also listen to gospel and inspirational music. The Bible is a book that I stand on, along with many other books that I have read. I also have had the pleasure of meeting people who have poured into my spirit what the Lord wants me to know. I encourage you to elevate your mind. As we go on this journey, we learn and grow. We must move forward.

Restoration from and reformation of abandonment issues and situations are necessary. Reform the people in jail. Reform the brokenness that entered your life after you were abandoned. Let God restore you back to your original state. Know that you can overcome even the most hurtful of situations. In the process, God will send complete strangers into your life to help you. They may be people who feel some sort of a connection to you. What they do is help you through without even knowing it. Victory is in sight! Again, we must move forward.

I began affirming who I was in Christ. I am beautiful. I am unique. I am love. I am at peace. I am awesome. I do believe it! Let's share our individual strengths and grow in grace. When we share, we help others along in their process, too. For example, there are some books that have helped me to heal, which in turn put a smile on my face. These books were written by other people who experienced the same things I have and then wrote their story. Your change will take the participation of other people. Therefore, you must surround yourself with people who want to support you. Open the door to your heart with the appropriate boundaries and trust people to be a part of your process. Be encouraged by these testimonies and process of overcoming. Don't let people judge you. Sometimes we are written off and not expected to be successful. Don't give up on your dreams and don't give up on yourself.

I was fortunate enough to attend Social Emotional Learning workshops through my job that really helped to support me in opening up and looking at the wounds I had due to abandonment issues. Having resources and outlets is important. Being able to share my pain and disappointment of losing my culture was the beginning of the healing. I learned a lot in my educational and spiritual school and no matter what, that is something that cannot be taken away. Restorative practices for well-being are important because we do so much every day.

The following are just a few of the books that I have read that have impacted my life and helped me to grow:

- *The Holy Bible*
- *The Lost Books of the Bible: Solomon J. Schepps Bell Publishing Company New York*

- *The Story of the Christian Church* by Jesse Lyman Hurlbut
- *19 Gifts of the Spirit* by Leslie B. Flynn
- *From Stress to Well-Being* by Craig Ellison
- *Pedagogy of the Oppressed* by Pablo Frier
- *Cultivating Genius* by Gholdy Muhammad

In addition to these books, I have read writings from many other authors, including Jacqueline Woodson and Toni Morrison, Warren W. Wiersbe. If you have recommendations of your own, don't wait for permission to come to the table. Bring what you have and share willingly for the progression of the universe.

There are so many books I have read. Yes, it is true: reading is informative and can make a significant impact on your life. I am working on a live podcast discussing this book, abandonment issues and other topics where we can share our thoughts and feelings for discovering solutions. After all of the things I have been through, I still have joy.

Something to Celebrate

We all have something to celebrate about ourselves as we learn and grow.

I am someone to celebrate. I celebrate myself. I celebrate all that I have overcome and accomplished and conquered to be where I am today. I had to show up and do the work. I never abandoned my dreams and I stood on the promises of God. Thank God, I am still working.

LOVE GROWS HERE!

About The Author

I am Jacqueline Scott. My life's experiences have taught me how to grow in God's grace and be the best me I can be. I am confident in what I have learned and that I can share my experiences and knowledge with others. Looking in the mirror is difficult sometimes. How do we see ourselves? I see a hard-working woman who has made some mistakes, but they do not define who I am.

I was adopted and worked hard to achieve my success. Nothing was just given to me. I wanted my life to go a certain way, but God is in control. I am grateful for my experiences and how I have overcome some of the most trying ones. I am more than a conqueror through Christ. I have obtained a Bachelor of Arts in Communications with a minor in Education from the College of New Rochelle in New York City with a GPA of 3.8. I also have a Master of Education from Cambridge College NITE program from Cambridge, Massachusetts with a 4.0 GPA. I am moving towards completing my final year at Manhattan Bible Institute.

I have a great career working for the New York City Department of Education for 23.3 years, where I have accumulated a portfolio with several professional development and workshop certificates. My spiritual journey has led me to become a certified chaplain. God has also allowed me to be elevated to a minister. However, amidst all of these accomplishments, my most heartfelt and special accomplishment is being a proud mother of four daughters, Alacea, Emkasia, Jasmond, and Monajae, and a grandmother of two handsome grandsons, Enrique, and Julian. This is why I am willing to share what I have learned through some of my life with you.

Conqueror Notes: _____

_____

_____

_____

_____

_____

_____

_____

_____

_____

_____

_____

_____

_____

_____

_____

_____

_____

_____

_____

_____

_____

_____

_____

_____

_____

_____

_____

_____

_____

Conqueror Notes: _____

_____

_____

_____

_____

_____

_____

_____

_____

_____

_____

_____

_____

_____

_____

_____

_____

_____

_____

_____

_____

_____

_____

_____

_____

_____

_____

_____

_____

_____

_____

Conqueror Notes: _____

_____

_____

_____

_____

_____

_____

_____

_____

_____

_____

_____

_____

_____

_____

_____

_____

_____

_____

_____

_____

_____

_____

_____

_____

_____

_____

_____

_____

_____

Conqueror Notes: _____

_____

_____

_____

_____

_____

_____

_____

_____

_____

_____

_____

_____

_____

_____

_____

_____

_____

_____

_____

_____

_____

_____

_____

_____

_____

_____

_____

_____

_____

Conqueror Notes: _____

_____

_____

_____

_____

_____

_____

_____

_____

_____

_____

_____

_____

_____

_____

_____

_____

_____

_____

_____

_____

_____

_____

_____

_____

_____

_____

_____

_____

_____

_____

Conqueror Notes: _____

_____

_____

_____

_____

_____

_____

_____

_____

_____

_____

_____

_____

_____

_____

_____

_____

_____

_____

_____

_____

_____

_____

_____

_____

_____

_____

_____

_____

_____

Conqueror Notes: _____

_____

_____

_____

_____

_____

_____

_____

_____

_____

_____

_____

_____

_____

_____

_____

_____

_____

_____

_____

_____

_____

_____

_____

_____

_____

_____

_____

_____

_____

Conqueror Notes: _____

_____

_____

_____

_____

_____

_____

_____

_____

_____

_____

_____

_____

_____

_____

_____

_____

_____

_____

_____

_____

_____

_____

_____

_____

_____

_____

_____

_____

Conqueror Notes: _____

_____

_____

_____

_____

_____

_____

_____

_____

_____

_____

_____

_____

_____

_____

_____

_____

_____

_____

_____

_____

_____

_____

_____

_____

_____

_____

_____

_____

_____

_____

_____

_____

Conqueror Notes: _____

_____

Conqueror Notes: _____

_____

_____

_____

_____

_____

_____

_____

_____

_____

_____

_____

_____

_____

_____

_____

_____

_____

_____

_____

_____

_____

_____

_____

_____

_____

_____

_____

_____

_____

_____

Conqueror Notes: _____

_____

_____

_____

_____

_____

_____

_____

_____

_____

_____

_____

_____

_____

_____

_____

_____

_____

_____

_____

_____

_____

_____

_____

_____

_____

_____

_____

_____

_____

_____

_____

_____

Conqueror Notes: _____

_____

_____
_____
_____
_____
_____
_____
_____
_____
_____
_____
_____
_____
_____
_____
_____
_____
_____
_____
_____
_____
_____
_____
_____
_____
_____
_____
_____
_____
_____
_____

Conqueror Notes: _____

_____
_____
_____
_____
_____
_____
_____
_____
_____
_____
_____
_____
_____
_____
_____
_____
_____
_____
_____
_____
_____
_____
_____
_____
_____
_____
_____
_____
_____
_____

Conqueror Notes: _____

_____

_____

_____

_____

_____

_____

_____

_____

_____

_____

_____

_____

_____

_____

_____

_____

_____

_____

_____

_____

_____

_____

_____

_____

_____

_____

_____

_____

_____

_____

_____

_____

_____

Conqueror Notes: _____

_____
_____
_____
_____
_____
_____
_____
_____
_____
_____
_____
_____
_____
_____
_____
_____
_____
_____
_____
_____
_____
_____
_____
_____
_____
_____
_____
_____
_____

Conqueror Notes: _____

_____

_____

_____

_____

_____

_____

_____

_____

_____

_____

_____

_____

_____

_____

_____

_____

_____

_____

_____

_____

_____

_____

_____

_____

_____

_____

_____

_____

_____

_____

_____

Conqueror Notes: _____

_____
_____
_____
_____
_____
_____
_____
_____
_____
_____
_____
_____
_____
_____
_____
_____
_____
_____
_____
_____
_____
_____
_____
_____
_____
_____
_____
_____

Conqueror Notes: _____

_____

_____

_____

_____

_____

_____

_____

_____

_____

_____

_____

_____

_____

_____

_____

_____

_____

_____

_____

_____

_____

_____

_____

_____

_____

_____

_____

_____

_____

_____

_____

Conqueror Notes: _____

_____

_____

_____

_____

_____

_____

_____

_____

_____

_____

_____

_____

_____

_____

_____

_____

_____

_____

_____

_____

_____

_____

_____

_____

_____

_____

_____

_____

Conqueror Notes: _____

_____

_____

_____

_____

_____

_____

_____

_____

_____

_____

_____

_____

_____

_____

_____

_____

_____

_____

_____

_____

_____

_____

_____

_____

_____

_____

_____

_____

_____

_____

_____

_____

Conqueror Notes: _____

_____

_____

_____

_____

_____

_____

_____

_____

_____

_____

_____

_____

_____

_____

_____

_____

_____

_____

_____

_____

_____

_____

_____

_____

_____

_____

_____

_____

Conqueror Notes: _____

_____

_____

_____

_____

_____

_____

_____

_____

_____

_____

_____

_____

_____

_____

_____

_____

_____

_____

_____

_____

_____

_____

_____

_____

_____

_____

_____

_____

_____

_____

_____

Conqueror Notes: _____

_____
_____
_____
_____
_____
_____
_____
_____
_____
_____
_____
_____
_____
_____
_____
_____
_____
_____
_____
_____
_____
_____
_____
_____
_____
_____
_____
_____

Conqueror Notes: _____

_____

_____

_____

_____

_____

_____

_____

_____

_____

_____

_____

_____

_____

_____

_____

_____

_____

_____

_____

_____

_____

_____

_____

_____

_____

_____

_____

_____

_____

Conqueror Notes: _____

_____
_____
_____
_____
_____
_____
_____
_____
_____
_____
_____
_____
_____
_____
_____
_____
_____
_____
_____
_____
_____
_____
_____
_____
_____
_____
_____
_____
_____

Conqueror Notes: _____

_____

_____

_____

_____

_____

_____

_____

_____

_____

_____

_____

_____

_____

_____

_____

_____

_____

_____

_____

_____

_____

_____

_____

_____

_____

_____

_____

_____

_____

_____

_____

_____

_____

Conqueror Notes: _____

_____

_____

_____

_____

_____

_____

_____

_____

_____

_____

_____

_____

_____

_____

_____

_____

_____

_____

_____

_____

_____

_____

_____

_____

_____

_____

_____

Conqueror Notes: _____

_____

_____

_____

_____

_____

_____

_____

_____

_____

_____

_____

_____

_____

_____

_____

_____

_____

_____

_____

_____

_____

_____

_____

_____

_____

_____

_____

_____

_____

_____

Conqueror Notes: _____

_____
_____
_____
_____
_____
_____
_____
_____
_____
_____
_____
_____
_____
_____
_____
_____
_____
_____
_____
_____
_____
_____
_____
_____
_____
_____
_____
_____
_____
_____
_____

Conqueror Notes: _____

_____

_____

_____

_____

_____

_____

_____

_____

_____

_____

_____

_____

_____

_____

_____

_____

_____

_____

_____

_____

_____

_____

_____

_____

_____

_____

_____

_____

_____

_____

_____

Conqueror Notes: _____

_____

_____

_____

_____

_____

_____

_____

_____

_____

_____

_____

_____

_____

_____

_____

_____

_____

_____

_____

_____

_____

_____

_____

_____

_____

_____

_____

_____

_____

_____

_____

_____

Conqueror Notes: _____

_____

_____

_____

_____

_____

_____

_____

_____

_____

_____

_____

_____

_____

_____

_____

_____

_____

_____

_____

_____

_____

_____

_____

_____

_____

_____

_____

_____

_____

_____

Conqueror Notes: _____

_____
_____
_____
_____
_____
_____
_____
_____
_____
_____
_____
_____
_____
_____
_____
_____
_____
_____
_____
_____
_____
_____
_____
_____
_____
_____
_____
_____
_____
_____

Conqueror Notes: _____

_____

_____

_____

_____

_____

_____

_____

_____

_____

_____

_____

_____

_____

_____

_____

_____

_____

_____

_____

_____

_____

_____

_____

_____

_____

_____

_____

_____

_____

_____

_____

_____

Conqueror Notes: _____

_____

_____

_____

_____

_____

_____

_____

_____

_____

_____

_____

_____

_____

_____

_____

_____

_____

_____

_____

_____

_____

_____

_____

_____

_____

_____

_____

_____

_____

Conqueror Notes: _____

_____

_____

_____

_____

_____

_____

_____

_____

_____

_____

_____

_____

_____

_____

_____

_____

_____

_____

_____

_____

_____

_____

_____

_____

_____

_____

_____

_____

_____

Conqueror Notes: _____

_____

_____

_____

_____

_____

_____

_____

_____

_____

_____

_____

_____

_____

_____

_____

_____

_____

_____

_____

_____

_____

_____

_____

_____

_____

_____

_____

_____

_____

_____

_____

Conqueror Notes: _____

_____

_____

_____

_____

_____

_____

_____

_____

_____

_____

_____

_____

_____

_____

_____

_____

_____

_____

_____

_____

_____

_____

_____

_____

_____

_____

_____

_____

CPSIA information can be obtained
at www.ICGtesting.com
Printed in the USA
BVHW042017171021
619165BV00013B/140

9 781942 871644